101 Nifty Ideas

For High Schools

By

Dr. William Reid

Illustrated by Keith Shaw

Published by ESP "WISE" Publications

For permission please contact: .

Sandi Redenbach, President
ESP "WISE" Publications
313 Del Oro Avenue, Davis, CA 95616
phone   530-756-8678   fax   530-756-5537
web site: www.espp.org
email: spopcorn@espp.org
800-354-6724

Table of Contents

Introduction

Like many fellow administrators, I am a regular participant in professional development activities. I also like to visit other schools. The difference between what I consider a good professional development activity and a poor one, or a good visit and a poor one can come down to one question.
"Did I find an idea I could take home and use in my school?"

Over the years, I have found many ideas for teaching and administration which I have been able to use, and of course, there are the numerous workshops on supervision, legalities, leadership, policy, report writing, and most recently, multiple intelligences, learning styles, and brain research. Now don't get me wrong. That's all important stuff, and I do consider myself a true lifelong learner - after all, I have completed some four degrees, and goodness know how many certificate programs.

However, I must confess that I get a true sense of pure satisfaction when I bring home an idea that I can readily implement in my school. And, I prefer simple ideas. Over the years, I have accumulated quite a list of easy to implement ideas. The ideas generally have one of several themes.
The themes are basically centered around the following:

1. **Marketing the school**: In these days, if your school does not brag about and celebrate its successes, and proclaim its worth, then no one else will. Schools have many detractors, often people who have never visited them. Someone once told me that when auto manufacturers create a commercial, they are doing it for two groups of people: potential new customers, and customers that have already purchased but like the psychic reward of seeing the product they have purchased being advertised again. It seems to me that very often in schools, we neglect the clients we serve. I think we need to advertise to our students about what we do right and well. In turn, they will talk to their parents and through them, the community.

2. **Motivating the students**: We must always do whatever we can to motivate students, to achieve high academic results, excel in sports, and/or simply stay in school. Gimmicks do not compensate for a caring, dedicated staff, but a series of simple ideas can contribute to an overall climate that is encouraging, warm, and connective.

3. **Developing and maintaining a positive culture:** A positive school culture does not appear magically overnight. It is the product of an over-all plan which can be quite involved and complicated. Often there are nifty ideas that can be easily implemented and which complement other efforts. They will pay off in a sense of school pride and belonging.

4. **Being efficient:** I'm always looking for an idea that makes my school operate more efficiently. There are lots of ideas available, but sometimes they are expensive. The ones I like are usually simple and easy to implement.

5. **Raising money:** Entire books could be written about this topic, and there are always new ideas coming along. Over the years, I have picked up a few ideas which I like because they give students opportunities for leadership, feature student talent, do not involve door-to-door sales, and have the potential to make good money.

6. **Building a sense of team in the staff:** As the size of a school staff increases, it becomes harder to develop a sense of team. Teachers have their own subject areas and classrooms and may not see some members of the staff very often. It can be easy in a high school to become isolationist. The challenge then becomes one of creating a cohesive team encouraged to pursue the philosophy and goals of the school. Any ideas that will work on that sense of belonging and teamwork are always welcome.

So, as you peruse the ideas in this book, I hope that, like an effective inservice day, you find at least one good idea that you can put to use in your school very soon. I am sure that you might have heard of some of the ideas before, but got out of the habit of using them. Maybe the book will be a little inspiration to

give a second try. And if you have an idea that you would like to share, please fill out this form and send it along to me for the sequel. I hope you enjoy this book and all of its great ideas.

Got a Nifty Idea? Have it included in a sequel to this publication.

Your name: _____ Phone: _____
School: _____
Address: _____
Brief description of your nifty idea: _____
_____
_____
_____
_____

Mail to: **Dr. William Reid**
              604 West Innes Street, Nelson, BC
              Canada, V1L 3J3
Or email to breid@netidea.com

Developing and maintaining
a positive culture

Nifty Idea 1

School History Collage

Go through some of the old yearbooks. Pick out pictures that have significance to the history of the school: opening, renovations famous events, etc. Write out the history of the school and put it together with pictures to create a collage or display for visitors and new students to read. Use a nice frame. You'll be surprised at the number of people who will take interest.

Nifty Idea 2

Benches in Hallways

There is nothing like a picnic style bench to give a sterile hallway a friendlier atmosphere. Have the woodwork class make benches as a class production line project using the plan provided or consider a commercial vendor. Here is a hint: look to buy a church pew without the accessories such as hymn book holders, if you want a high quality solid wood product. Remember, the better the product looks, the more students will respect and maintain them.

Nifty Idea 3

Plants in the Hallway

Another means of de-sterilizing the hallways of a high school is to hang plants or place them on the floor in convenient locations. In three years of having plants in a variety of locations, we have only had one incident where a plant was knocked over. Watering and horticultural care are under the auspices of the special education department and some of our most challenged students have a routine of plant maintenance as part of their life skills program.

Nifty Idea 4

Principal's Choice Artwork

Pick a spot near or in the school office where students, staff, and parents will see a painting. Buy (or borrow) an easy-change frame and arrange with your art teacher to place a piece of student work in the frame. Pick out a piece by visiting the art class. Above or below the picture have a sign that says, "Principal's Choice". Change the picture weekly. Enjoy the look on the kid's face when their picture is selected. Put up two sometimes.

9

Nifty Idea 5

August Warning Letter

Sometimes the seniors in a school can get a little excited the weekend before school starts. Head off potential problems by sending out a letter to all students and their parents. Go over the rules and expectations for the school year and call upon the seniors to set a good tone for themselves in both the school and the community. Sending the letter will generate discussion between students and parents in most families which will save some potential first day problems.

11

Nifty Idea 6

Girls' Day in the Gym

You may find that a Girls Only day brings out some people to the gym at noon hour who normally wouldn't come out for a variety of reasons. Teenagers are often selfconscious about themselves and a little extra effort or promotion could go a long way towards encouraging gym use by someone who normally does not visit the gym. Consider a variety of activities: aerobics, intra-murals, free gym, practice, dance.

Run on the Vending Machine

High schools often have vending machines. If you have a contest and are wondering what to do for a prize, announce that the prize is a shopping spree on the vending machines. Stack up a pile of quarters on a table and on the far side of the room from the machines. Allow a time limit, one or two minutes, and let students take a maximum of $1.00 to the machines on each run. You'll find that students share the winnings with their friends.

Nifty Idea 8

Promote a Study Method

Students often find tests and exams to be stressful parts of the schooling process. We can do a lot for students if we teach them a method of study such as SQ3R (Survey, Question, Read, Recite, Review) or similar method. Posting rules for study and referring to them before each test reinforces the need for a systematic approach to study. Teachers can modify to meet the needs of their particular curriculum and relate personal tips and suggestions. By being exposed to a variety, students will be able to select from a variety of suggestions and hopefully, find ones that work well for them.

Give Halloween Back to the Kids

Halloween used to be a rough night for the local police until we developed a program with them in which the high school seniors are paired up with youngsters in the community who need an older friend to take them trick-or-treating. There are several results: the grads are pumped up with the responsibility of making the night safe for young kids; they are gainfully employed; they have helped out the single parent families; and the public relations for the class within the community is huge. And now, the grads are asking when they can sign up for the next year.

19

Nifty Idea 10

Mirrors in the hallways

Install a full length mirror inside the entrance doors. High school kids like to check their hair and make sure that everything is in order.

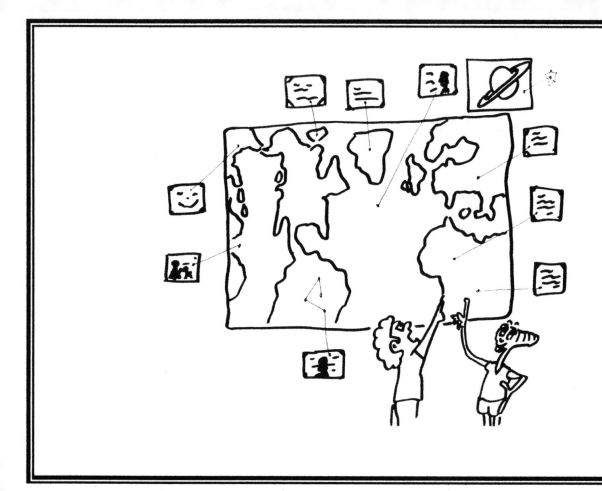

Nifty Idea 11

Map display for exchange students

A local service club may be willing to purchase an enclosed wall-display cabinet for the school to hold a world map and display pictures of where exchange students were born and where students from the school have visited. A distance indicator shows how far from home the students are.

23

Nifty Idea 12

New student bulletin board

Got new kids midyear? Create a bulletin board display. With a Polaroid camera, snap a few pictures. Make up a sheet with some simple information: first name, grade, from where, favorite TV show, favorite music, favorite sports, favorite subjects.

Nifty Idea 13

Professional Development for Kids: Superhost; Self-Defense; Job Fair

During the school year, we often organize professional development activities for the staff. Consider offering sessions for the students too. A one-day course in self-defense goes over really well with students and parents. It's easy to organize and often the local police department will let a community liaison officer deliver the program. Other ideas include certificate programs such as "Superhost," "food safe" or crafts, theater, or painting.

Nifty Idea 14

Christmas room decorating contest

Have the student council organize a room-decorating contest for the holiday season. Offer a prize such as a pizza party for the room judged to be best decorated. You may wish to create some rules about the decorations: eg. must be handmade, etc.

Nifty Idea 15

Flags of Countries

Schools usually enjoy a wide cross-section of ethnic backgrounds. Celebrate the countries of origin by putting a small flag up in the hall to represent each country of ancestry for the students of the school. You'll have a colorful display and continuous testimonial to the unique heritage which makes a country great.

Nifty Idea 16

Student Council Bulletin Board

Consider installing a special bulletin board for your student council. We installed a nice oakboard that featured three glass doors. Messages, special notes, and pictures can safely be placed in the cabinet. It doesn't take long for students to learn that they should check the special board for the latest student council news.

33

Nifty Idea 17

Picture of Student Council

Use your student council cabinet to display a picture of the executive early in the school year. Schools usually have school pictures of all students. Have some blown up to a 5 X 7 size. Put names under the pictures and add a title that says, "Get to Know Your Student Government"

Nifty Idea 18

Picture of Grad Committee

High schools usually have a graduation club or council which organizes activities related to the graduation. Put up a picture of the main committee members in the main entrance with a few notes about their duties related to the graduation. Five by seven pictures work well. It gives the working members a little recognition, and in large schools allows the senior class to put a name to the face.

Nifty Idea 19

PicNic Tables

If you don't already have picnic tables for the students for the nicer days of spring and fall, please consider them. A classic design can be built relatively cheaply. A few years of use and they can be replaced. If money allows, buy ones built with exposed aggregate concrete and they will last forever. Add a splash of color by putting umbrellas in the centers. Remember to bring the umbrellas in at night though.

Nifty Idea 20

Hacky-sack Contest

Most schools have rules prohibiting the use of hacky-sacks in the building because walls eventually get scuffed up and require painting. A fun tournament, which acknowledges the hacky- sackers and gives them a legitimate audience for their game is worthwhile in terms of school spirit. Pick some judges and base the contest upon who can keep the hacky sack in the air longest. Run individual as well as team competitions.

Nifty Idea 21

Student Art-Work Display

High school art rooms are often filled with displays of student work. We turned our hallways into year round art galleries by installing wooden strips which make it easy to hang student work in easy-access frames. The fours-inch boards are mounted permanently on the walls at eye level. The groove in the center of the board makes it easy to insert a holder which is safe. On a piece of paper under the artwork, place the student's name and the title of the piece.

Statement of Philosophy

We focus on excellence in a nurturing environment in which all student are created equal and the whole child is the focus of our intense endeavors to create a human being that will contribute in a meaningful way to our society as a whole and yadda yadda yadda and so on and so forth and etc. . . . . you know what we mean!

Nifty Idea 22

Statement Of Philosophy Framed

High schools always have a statement of philosophy, but it is sometimes hard to find as it collects dust. Print it out neatly, frame it, and hang it in the main entrance so that everyone has access to it. Keep your philosophy in front of your staff and students.

Nifty Idea 23

Use a Banner

Buy a banner with the school logo and team name on it. A simple eight or ten foot banner can go with teams to tournaments or be displayed at the local field when the team is playing or in the community whenever there is a school fund-raiser. It will instill pride in the team and serve as an identification during a tournament for fans and players alike. Banners are inexpensive and last a long time.

Nifty Idea 24

New Student Welcome Day

Fire up the barbecue and cook hamburgers and hot dogs for students new to the school on a warm September day. Have the senior students or the staff do the cooking. Give a ticket to each student new to the building, and sell tickets to anyone else who wants a barbecued burger. You'll create some good will with those new to the school and have organized an activity that makes them feel at home.

Nifty Idea 25

Encourage A Legacy

It started off with wondering what to do with some funds left over from fundraising for graduation activities. A donation was made to a local cause, a puppet theater for the public library. From that point on, it became part of what was done, a donation as part of the legacy of the graduating class. They can come up with the ideas. There are always good uses for funding and excellent ways to remember a graduating class.

Our Code of Ethics

- All Teachers respect the 'Human Rights' of all students at all times as stated in the United Nation's Charter of Basic Rights and Freedoms including the right to Self Determination and Democracy within the Classroom = Unless this interferes with the Teacher's Ability to control the class.

Nifty Idea 26

Post the Code of Ethics

Professional groups such as teachers usually adhere to a code of ethics. Arrange with teachers to have the code posted in each classroom. It serves several purposes. First, it is a reminder to everyone about the code of behavior required of teachers. Secondly, it serves as a model for student behavior. It reminds students that they have rights and everyone can benefit from well-defined rules of conduct.

School T-Shirt

Have students design the school T-shirt for that year. Encourage creativity by offering a small prize to the winning design. Sell as many T-shirts as students are willing to pre-order. Look for a design that encourages achievement or suggests that the school is a great place to learn.

Nifty Idea 28

A Gift at Christmas

You'll delight every student and staff member in the building if you give out a small gift just before the Christmas holiday. You may consider a school pen or key chain. Put the school logo on whatever it is. I am never disappointed by the smiles on kids' faces when they see that you have been thinking of them. Leftovers? Give to new students as they appear during the year as a sign of welcome.

Theater Sports Night

Theater Sports is one of the funniest forms of drama. It is a type of improvisation, but based upon certain games with rules. Your drama teacher will be familiar with theater sports. Put on a theater sports night in conjunction with a spaghetti dinner and you'll create a great evening for students and parents. Theater sports are easy to organize, and the laughs will be non-stop.

"STOP HARASSMENT WEEK"
I Pledge to:
Not bother, harass bug, interfere with or in any way cause harm to another person in the school during school hours
Signed ARNOLD
I Pledge to:
Never again to use my over-powering strength to gain advantage over another person. Except in Sports!
Guy Toughman
I Pledge
Stop hara
Everywher
School Prin
Apologise
Toe-Hold
Barb Wire

Nifty Idea 30

Anti-Harassment Week

Early in the year, set up a display with the co-operation of your student leaders in which harassment is defined and proper ways to treat people are outlined. Arrange for large sheets of paper to be available for students to sign, pledging with their signature to be part of a harassment-free school. At the end of the week mount the large sheets somewhere where they can be seen by everyone. You'll have an incredible visual display and a constant reminder that you support a nurturing environment.

Put Assignments and Tests on the Board

Encourage your teachers to assign a small section of the board as an area where they list the assignments due and test dates for each class. It's a great habit because it serves as a reminder for the students. The next step would be to put an outline on the board for the day's lesson plan. Work on the tests and assignments first.

Motivating the students

Nifty Idea 32

Birthday Pen/Pencil

Get a list of whose birthday is when and give kids a school pen or pencil on their birthday. Depending upon the size of the school, you could deliver by hand, or have kids pick one up in the office, or have a few on you at all times and let kids stop you in the halls. You never know, for some kids, it might be the only present they get.

Nifty Idea 33

Just a Smile

Encourage staff, and don't forget yourself, to smile and say "hi" to kids in the hall. For some, it might be the only positive interaction they have with another human being that day. You'll never know the difference it makes, but it costs you nothing. Fill up an emotional bucket; don't drain it.

Nifty Idea 34

Good News From School Letters and Letterhead

Every school has formal letterhead. For this nifty idea, print up some letterhead with the logo and name at the bottom. In a semi-circle across the top print "Good News From School." Use the letterhead whenever you can for honor roll recognition, successful election to student council, special achievement, etc. Imagine the smile on a parent's face when they open a letter from the school and the first thing they read is "Good News." Be prepared to be stopped on the street as parents offer their thanks to you.

Nifty Idea 35

Principal's Honor Roll

Most schools have an honor roll which recognizes students with a "B" or better GPA. Try instituting a principal's honor roll for those with a GPA of 3.5 or better. It provides an additional incentive for students who are achievers and want something to take aim at and so it is a simple way to provide some motivation.

Nifty Idea 36

Citizenship Award Roll

Schools often recognize the academic and talented. But there are a lot of solid students who go unrecognized. Institute a major award such as a wall plaque for citizenship and recognize one of those students who is known in the school as an exemplary citizen. Give a certificate to anyone else nominated.

Nifty Idea 37

Work Ethic List

It's easy to recognize students who achieve honor roll standing. But there is another large clientele who work very hard to get a "C" or "C+". Give them credit if their teachers recognize their work ethic by creating a list of those who achieve a commendation from five of their eight teachers. Many schools have a means of assessing work habits with a "G" (Good), "S" (Satisfactory), and "N" (Needs Improvement). Use it!

Nifty Idea 38

Student Of The Week

Pick a student each week or month to receive recognition for effort or achievement. Publicize the winner on the local radio station or newspaper. You may find that one of the local restaurants will provide some sponsorship for a small prize.

Nifty Idea 39

Wall Plaques for Citizenship, Improvement and Best All-Around

If you recognize the school's top students at an awards day, consider having a plaque in the main hallway to honor them and record them in the school's history. Try recognizing your best citizen and most improved student as well as the top all-around student. You'll be recognizing more than academics and sports and will open up awards to another group of students.

Scholarship: Student Government President

Consider giving a scholarship to your student government president. It does not have to be a lot of money, but even a small amount will recognize the time, efforts and leadership provided to the student body in a way that can be used on a resume or simply recorded in the school files. The money, of course will be spent on further education and has therefore gone to a good cause.

Nifty Idea 41

Turn Off The Bells

Want to take some stress out of the school day? Turn off the bells. I think schools are about the only institutions which use a bell to give a warning that another bell is going to ring to signal that attendance will be taken in a homeroom five minutes before another bell rings to start class. Turn them off. Let the kids use their watches the same way they would to start a part-time job or go to a movie. End the Pavlovian conditioning. It will take a bit of time to get used to, but you'll grow to like it fast.

NEW TIMETABLE

8:45 AM	10:30 PM	6:15 LTD	12:20 AM
BLOCK A	BLOCK C	BLOCK L	H&R BLOCK
MATH	**SCIENCE**	**ENGLASH**	**MUSIC**
11:30 MONDAY	TUESDAY ONLY	ODD NUMBERED WEEKS	MONTHS WITH AN "L"
BIOLOGY	**LUNCH**	**MATH**	**SCILENCE**
TWO DAYS FOLLOWING A NATIONAL HOLIDAY	IF IT'S ALSO GARBAGE DAY	DAY OFF IF SUBSTITUTE TEACHER	IF I FORGOT TO GO TO CLASS, GO NOW!
ART	**COMPUTER SCIENCE**	**P.E.**	**FRENCH**

83

Nifty Idea 42

Timetable

Entire books and dissertations have been written about timetables. I know. I wrote one of them. If you haven't looked at block scheduling or the Copernican Plan, please do. You don't have to buy into an entire system, but a modification to what you presently do might create possibilities for kids that you haven't thought of. Our timetable change enabled many things including outstanding programs in adventure tourism, value-added wood, carpentry, recreational leadership, and work experience. And all the while the school maintained an exceptional academic record.

Arrange an Exchange

To give teachers a break and a change if they are interested, arrange an exchange with a neighboring school district. Allow your teachers to visit another school, or couple of schools to see programs and teaching ideas. Encourage the other school to visit in return. Use inservice funds to pay for the substitute teachers. If the district is quite far away, consider a billeting between the staffs. You'll be impressed by the level of energy and number of ideas created by an exchange and the new energy passed on to the students.

Nifty Idea 44

Special Days: 1897 Day

Go back over 100 years in time for a nifty idea that provides a school-wide theme that is educational and fun. Dress appropriately with prizes for best costume, use the old rules for a day, research schooling, use slates in math, have a student run up the halls with a hand bell, print a special newspaper, have a spelling bee, hold a handwriting competition, run an antique picture booth, and showcase the whole works with an open house for parents and community.

Nifty Idea 45

The Welcoming Sign

I don't know how many schools I've been in where the first sign you see upon entering is a sign extolling visitors to check in at the office. I've always found that sign a little cold. A much better sign is the one we mounted welcoming everyone and stating, "great students, great staff . . . great school." The sign has a very brief summary of what we do well: academics, fine arts, athletics, and technology. The sign was made by students in a technology class but could have been purchased.

Nifty Idea 46

Senior Exam Study Night

Exams are stressful for students, especially the seniors if they have to write a state or provincial exam. We can help them out if we offer an evening or Saturday study session. A bit of money allows the purchase of pizza for a light lunch or drinks and cookies for a snack. Students will appreciate the efforts of the teachers and parents will appreciate the dedication.

Take Student Leaders On A Tour Of Other Schools

It's common for students to visit other schools as members of a school team, but uncommon to visit to see another school in session. Take your student government leaders on a three school tour one day. Make the arrangements in advance of course. Visit classes and meet with other school leaders about activities and special events that work. Take your kids out for lunch. Be prepared to have a group of excited teenagers when you get home.

95

Nifty Idea 48

Always Have Kids Start Teacher Professional Development Days

Has your district committee organized a Professional Development day for teachers? Ask to have your school band or theater sports team warm up the audience, or at least play while people are entering the auditorium. You'll be giving your group an opportunity to perform on stage, enhancing the professional day, and putting out that all-important message about how good your school is. You can never put the message out enough.

Nifty Idea 49

Work Experience Before Drop Out

Despite your best efforts, some students will place themselves in a position where you have to ask them to leave school. Before taking that last, final step try putting the student out on a school sponsored work experience. The student can get a sense of the world of work and you'll have the satisfaction of knowing that something better is being done than walking the streets. Let the student know that, when they are ready for school, the door will be open.

Nifty Idea 50

Wall of Fame

This project takes a lot of time and effort, but the end result is worth the work. Start by writing to community service clubs, and groups asking for nominations for the school's wall of fame. Look for people who graduated and went on to become leaders in industry, politics, sciences, military, sports, etc. Have a committee of students, parents, and staff select candidates to the wall of fame. Do a write-up and get a picture. Put it all together in a nice frame. Hold a dedication evening. Reserve one frame and write "Future Wall of Famers - - Will this be you?"

Scholarship Wall

All schools have students who win achievements such as scholarships. But not all schools take advantage of the opportunity to recognize the ongoing achievements of students by creating a scholarship wall. Create one in your school using nice frames and good paper with neat printing or a nice computer font to publicize the scholarship achievement of students. You will find that you've created an atmosphere of achievement and benchmarks for future students.

103

Nifty Idea 52

Remembrance Day Assembly: candle lighting ceremony

Every school should have an assembly before Remembrance Day, but often deciding the program is difficult. Our program became easy the year we lit a candle for each of our graduates who died in service to their country. A candle is placed and lit in a holder we made out of wood and covered with tin foil while a poppy is placed to the reading of each name. The choir hums "Amazing Grace," breaking into song as the last name is recited and then sings one complete verse before two minutes of silence. We never cease to be amazed at the power of the assembly.

Nifty Idea 53

Donut Day

When our school went through a major renovation, students often put up with less than perfect learning conditions. There were noises, detours, smells, temperature variations, and alternate sites. When an area was renovated, we would buy donuts for every student in the school and the administrators would go from class to class handing them out. It was an easy way to thank students for their patience and understanding.

Nifty Idea 54

Plaque In Memory Of

If a student passes away during the school year, you may wish to consider a small plaque honoring the student. For students who knew the deceased, it helps with closure knowing that the memory of their friend continues. The plaque may contain a list of the student's memorable qualities or a brief life summary.

Nifty Idea 55

Student Crime Stoppers Program With Cash Rewards

Going through a bad time with theft or vandalism? Try a student crime-stopper program. Often the community crime stoppers will help with a school-based program. A few signs around the school about things that have gone missing might bring enough tips to put you on the right track to eliminating the problem. At the very least, you'll raise awareness and that by itself may reduce theft and vandalism.

Nifty Idea 56

Cotton-Candy Grams

Two weeks before Valentine's Day, pre-sell "cotton-candy grams" with a Valentine's message for a friend. Charge a couple of dollars. On Valentine's Day, rent a cotton candy machine and make up the cotton candy. Deliver it to the recipients just before lunchtime. As principal, pick 20 kids who wouldn't expect it, and send them a candy gram signed anonymous. Do the same thing at Christmas with candy canes.

Nifty Idea 57

Blow ball Tournament

Looking for something different during a long winter? Organize a BlowBall tournament. Teams of four students compete against each other. Use a Ping-Pong table, but any type of table will do. Put a piece of masking tape across the center of the table. Teams kneel on either side of the table. Players place their hands behind their backs and a ping- pong ball is dropped on the center of the table. The object of the game is to blow the ball off the other team's side of the table. First team to get to seven , wins. Have prizes for the tournament winners. This is a lot of fun to watch.

Nifty Idea 58

Jive is Alive Night

If you are in a smaller district and far from a major center, you know how expensive it is to bring in special people such as professional musicians to give your band students a quality workshop. Hold a Jive-Is-Alive Night which features select numbers performed by your area schools. If there are four schools in the area and each plays for 15 minutes you'll have the basis for a concert. Add in a set by the professional you bring in from the big city and you've got a night to remember. Use the proceeds from the concert to pay the required expenses. Have the professional join in with each school band for one or two numbers. It will bring out the best in the kids.

Nifty Idea 59

Your Own Television Station

This is a bit more ambitious, but easily within the realm of possibility. Instead of doing announcements over the PA system, establish your own television station. You'll need a television in each room, a camera in a central location and some student "anchors" to relate the news. Roving reporters can provide clips about school activities. We started out with televisions donated by a local hotel that was upgrading and donated cameras. Now we offer multi-media courses.

Marketing the school

Nifty Idea 60

Local Radio On-Site

Local radio stations are often big boosters of schools and you might be surprised at how economical a series of radio ads can be. Organize a day for the station to be on-site. Arrange for some students and teachers to do a 30 second clip on a theme such as: new curricula, focus on activities, academic success, why school's great. You get the idea. Don't be surprised if you get stopped in the grocery store by someone who heard you on the radio.

Team Summaries in Local Paper

You can create a nice piece of publicity by having a picture and a write-up of how school teams did throughout the year. Take out an ad (or see if the community newspaper will donate the space) and put a thumbnail size (2" by 1.5") of each team in the paper. Beside each team, put a brief notation as to how the team did: tournament winners; city champions; zone champions; second in league, etc. Not only do you have a nice summary in the media, but you've also got a summary for the school files.

123

Nifty Idea 62

Newsletters at Local Grocery Stores

High schools have a notoriously hard time getting school newsletters home to parents. Try putting some at the local grocery stores. Meet with the manager and arrange to have the newsletters available at the checkouts. Make sure the newsletters have a splashy headline so that more than just the parents take an interest.

Nifty Idea 63

Pens And Coffee Mugs For Special Guests

Schools often have guest speakers for assemblies or classrooms. We have found it to be a nice gesture to present the speaker with a school pen in a gift box or a school coffee mug. By buying them in bulk and letting staff know of their availability, you make it easy for all staff to show their appreciation for guests. The gift box need only be cardboard, but if it is a gold color, it will look nice.

Phone notification system

Computer programs such as PNS make it easy to import data from the administrative system and use that data for a call out to parents about special events such as parent night. Be a Good Samaritan to other schools. Allow them to record a variety of messages and plug in their parents' numbers for them. Activate the system when they need to send a message home. Are you more ambitious? As a fund-raiser, offer to set up a callout system for local groups such as service clubs who need to call members about meetings or projects. Input their membership for, say 25 cents a person and make the local calls for them for 10 cents each.

Local Lions Club

Scholarship

Past winners:
1990 Bob
1991 Sally
1992 Rex
1993 John
1994 Bill

Proud of our kids and our School

Nifty Idea 65

Scholarship results in community

Schools often have businesses and community groups that donate scholarships to the school to promote further education of the graduates. Prepare a framed list of the recipients of the particular business or group's past ten recipients. Attend a meeting to present the list. Ask them to hang it with pride in the place of business or meeting. You get the school promoted all year round. The group gets recognition. Use a frame in which it is easy to change the list. Offer an updated list yearly.

Nifty Idea 66

Art work in community

Get your students art work into the community where the young artists will have exposure to the general public. Approach doctors and dentists and see if you can hang framed artwork in their offices. Consider you city hall, and any other office buildings you can. You'll be pleased with the results.

Nifty Idea 67

Issue A Press Release

Place the phone numbers for your local media (newspaper, radio, and television) in your database. Get in the habit of making a news release a regular habit. Name yourself as the contact. Whether it is an academic result, a sports win, a new program, or a special achievement, send it in. Write is up as a news story: who what when where why. You'll find it ends up being printed on the slower news days. You'll also have a good connection in the event that there is bad news and you'll get called first. Don't expect everything to get in the news, but do expect results.

Nifty Idea 68

Coffee with the Principal

This is a great idea, and especially if you are new to a school. Set a time when parents can come in and have coffee with the principal. Arrange for every Friday at 10:00 am. Notify parents through the school newsletter. You'll find that not everyone can come on a school day, but some people can and will. Take advantage of the chance to get to know some parents and learn about their hopes and aspirations for their children. If there are any issues, you will hear about them too. The parents who can't attend will still appreciate the efforts to be open to parents.

Nifty Idea 69

University Counsellors at night.

It is common for schools to organize visits by local university and college counsellors who meet with students during the school day. We have had more success with their sessions since we switched them to the evening and invited parents. For the first time, parents and students can meet with the counsellors and learn about programs. It is our most successful evening, often with over 50% attendance from parents, an unusually high number for a high school

Scholarship Meeting night for parents

Schools with graduating students usually have a scholarship program to promote further education and reward excellence. We used to give out the scholarship information to students after an assembly, but found we had much more success with a scholarship meeting night where the parents and students came together and learned about the variety of scholarships available through colleges, universities, and local donors. Parents especially are appreciative of administrative efforts in hosting such an evening.

Nifty Idea 71

Barbecue for Parent Helpers

As the school year draws to a close, why not have a barbecue for those parents who gave a lot of time and energy to the school. Host it at someone's house (the principal's?) and keep the menu simple. Hamburgers, salad and a baked potato will do. Say a few words of praise and thank you. Ask for input about the following year's activities.

Being efficient

143

Nifty Idea 72

Recycling Centers

Here's a nifty idea for a garbage container that looks tidy and allows students to recycle their cans and bottles. A cardboard flat fits nicely inside the top. The front is hinged and holds a plastic garbage can on the inside. The design also allows for easier cleaning of the floors as a broom will slide smoothly underneath.

Spills and Misses Clipboard

Schools can set up a simple and efficient means of communicating between teaching staff and the custodial staff who are often busy and stretched and sometimes unaware of specific problems. A colored clip board, hung on the wall near the light switch and labeled "Spills and Misses" allows the classroom teacher to have a specific place to leave notes about the student who spilled or the burnt out light that was missed.

Nifty Idea 74

Recycled textbook covers

Schools go through a lot of paper. They can use the wrappers of the 500 sheet packages as textbook covers. They are the exact size required for a full-sized textbook, and are much better recipients of student doodling than the textbooks themselves. So save those wrappers.

149

Nifty Idea 75

Monday morning staff Meetings

Monthly staff meetings getting bogged down with trivia and organizational items which prevent discussion of more substantive issues? Hold a meeting first thing each Monday morning before class. Use it to go over the week's events and celebrate successes by teams or clubs from the previous week. Free up your monthly meeting for more important issues.

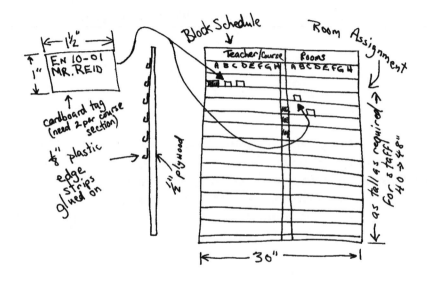

1½"

EN 10-01
MR. REID

1"

↑
cardboard tag
(need 2 per course
section)

⅛" plastic
edge
strips
glued on →

½" plywood

Block Schedule

Teacher/Course   Rooms
A B C D E F G H   A B C D E F G H

as tall as required →
for staff
40 → 48"

Room Assignment

|← 30" →|

Nifty Idea 76

Build Your Own Timetable Board

Secondary school master schedules are complicated. Some schools use a computer program to develop the master schedule and then schedule students while others develop the master schedule by hand and then let the computer program the students. If you build the master schedule by hand, then this design for a building board may be of interest. By using materials available in any building supply store, you can build this model, which allows you to track room usage as well as the teacher schedule by block. Light cardboard in a variety of colors serves as the tags for each course and section.

please post for whole family

This Term

Parent Night   Sept. 2
Soccer Game   Sept. 3
Picture Day   Sept. 4
Inservice Day   Sept. 5
Volleyball   Sept. 6
Cross Country   Sept. 7
Band Concert   Sept. 8
Drama night   Sept. 9

Go Rovers
www.rovers.com

and so on....

Continued on next page

Nifty Idea 77

Issue a Quarterly Calendar

It's always a good idea to let parents know what is when at the school. In addition to the regular newsletters, issue a quarterly calendar with specific dates for all the various events in the school. This calendar should also go to your Board Office and other schools in the district. It won't hurt to send a copy by fax to your local paper. You never know when a slow news day will result in a reporter taking in your event.

AWARDS CRITERIA

SEAGULL AWARD $10,000

SCHOLARSHIP

Open to all students of mixed MAYAN Finish Parents with B+ AVERAGE

CNNET TV BURSARY AWARD $10.50

SCHOLARSHIP

MUST MAINTAIN A A+ AVERAGE FOR 36 CONSECUTIVE MONTHS.

BASKET BALL OF FAME

HOOPS OF FUN DUNK 2000 CONSECUTIVE BASKETS GET 2 FREE SCHOOL DONUTS ON THE NEXT DONUT DAY OPEN TO ALL

Nifty Idea 78

Display Of Awards Available And Criteria

Schools usually have a system of awards for student achievement. It is a good idea to have a display of the awards available and how they can be earned. Surprisingly, students tend to achieve greater results when they know how high the bar is for the achievement.

Nifty Idea 79

Garbage Picker-Uppers

Sometimes a school will have students pick up garbage around the building as a consequence for misbehavior. This may work in some situations, but schools might create a more positive environment by having everyone participate in clean up. One of the problems with cleanups is picking up yucky garbage. You can solve the problem by purchasing some nifty picker-uppers. Picking up becomes easy and no-one minds pitching in. Picker-uppers are available from dealers of janitorial supplies.

Nifty Idea 80

Suggestion Box

It's a simple idea, and one often seen in businesses. Put up a suggestion box on the front counter of the office. You probably won't get a lot of suggestions, but you'll get some and they'll be good ones. What's better is that every student know that there is an opportunity for them to share their ideas, even if they choose not to.

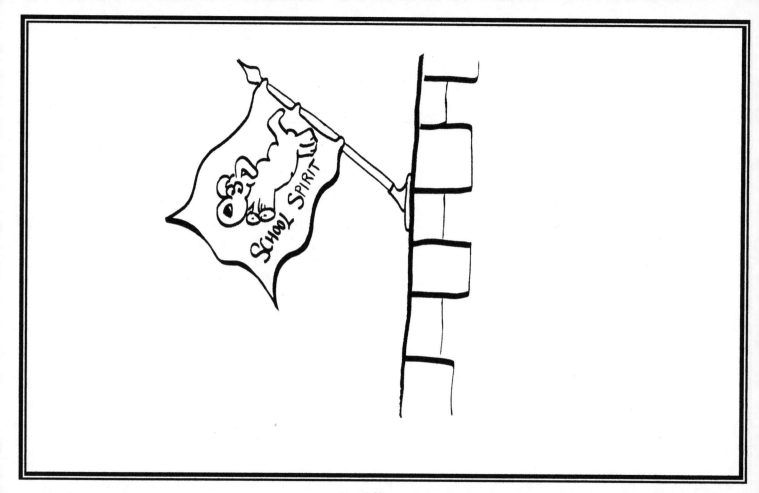

Nifty Idea 81

A Better flagpole

Schools always have a flagpole located on the grounds, but often the flag will be stolen if left out overnight. This simple flagpole design, mounted on the front of the school is more resistant to theft. Have your maintenance department construct it out of metal and mount it permanently.

Nifty Idea 82

Ice Packs

Often, in a high school, the kids will come to the office looking for an ice pack because they have sprained an ankle, wrist, or finger. It can be quite a chore to keep a supply of proper ice packs and since they seem to disappear, schools often use paper cups to make fast ice packs. However, they are not really that effective. A better solution is to buy a large box of latex medical gloves. Fill a glove with water, tie the end and put it in the freezer. The next morning you will have a cheap and effective, disposable ice pack.

Parking Registration

Got students who drive to school? Register their cars if you don't already. It will make life easier if you ever have to deal with complaints. You don't need a fancy, expensive system. Just create a form asking for information and enter it in a computer database. The very fact that you collect the information will make the students better drivers.

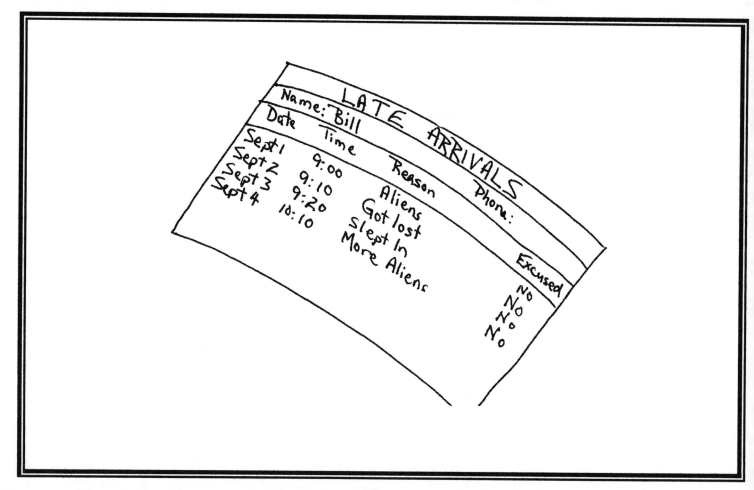

167

Nifty Idea 84

Card Late System

In these days of massive computer data collection and tracking abilities, a simple card system may still be the most effective way of dealing with student tardies. We make up a 5 by 8 card for each student at the beginning of the school year. On one side, they sign in late; on the back they indicate if they are leaving early. If they reach five lates, the card is flagged by the attendance clerk who turns it over to a vice- principal. The student receives a detention and a letter goes home with a copy of the card. No more silly sign-ins.

www.ourschool.org

Nifty Idea 85

Get a Web Site

It is hard to imagine secondary schools without a web site these days, but some still don't understand the importance of this new technology. If you've got kids in your school, you've got the expertise to get a web site going. An old computer will do, and if you use Linux software (which is free) as the operating system, costs will be minimal. Let the kids loose.

Put your newsletters and calendar on the web site.

171

Important Dates for the Year: At Front Entrance!

After the school calendar is set for the year, place a copy at the front entrance and one in the waiting area of the office. You'll find that you can never have this information available enough, and simple locations such as these may save a phone call or two, which take up valuable time.

Prior Arrangement Form

If you've ever gone through situations where students with planned absences did not know what work had to be made up or disagreed with their teachers about the arrangements for a make-up test, then you'll like the "prior arrangement form." By using it for planned absences, you'll have a record of parent request, work to be made up and plans for the make-up tests or quizzes. You'll also be able to indicate whether the absence is excused or unexcused.

Nifty Idea 88

Student Phone

A student phone located in a visible area near the main office will save wear and tear of the secretaries and the school phones. Be sure and tell the telephone company to restrict long distance access. See if the student council will pay the monthly charge and then put up a small sign letting student users know that they are the owners of the phone. For long distance calls, consider a pay phone. The school should get a cash return based upon the usage. Contact your local phone company for more details.

Raising money

Nifty Idea 89

Grad Fashion Show

If the graduation committee is looking to raise money, tell them to put on a fashion show. Get some parents to help. You'll find there is lots of fashion expertise in the school. Get some MC's, borrow the clothing (a contract with local stores is a good idea), put together some music. Families love a fashion show. Enhance the profits by hosting a silent auction the same night. Make sure there are adults backstage to ensure the clothes get back onto the proper hangers.

179

Nifty Idea 90

Host a Local Celebrity Game

Another great source of publicity is the celebrity sports game. Whether it's basketball, baseball, volleyball or some other sport, you can bet that there are local citizens who excelled at one time. Usually there are a few professional athletes in town that will chip in. Arrange for a game with the school team against the celebrities. Invite local dignitaries to play. Advertise well, have door prizes and a concession. Raise money for a local cause such as the hospital and take pride in the school spirit created. Supply ice packs for the celebrities. The kids will make them play to a level they have not achieved in years.

Grad Talent Show

Is your graduation committee looking for a fundraising idea. Hold a "Grad Talent Show." Give the students with talent an opportunity to perform by signing up. Rent a theater, or use the gym. Not enough kids in Grade 12 alone? Call upon the talents of next year's grad class, or the previous year's class if they are still around town. Charge $5.00. Have a couple of students act as MC's. Ask the drama teacher to give them a few pointers. You get the idea . . . run with it.

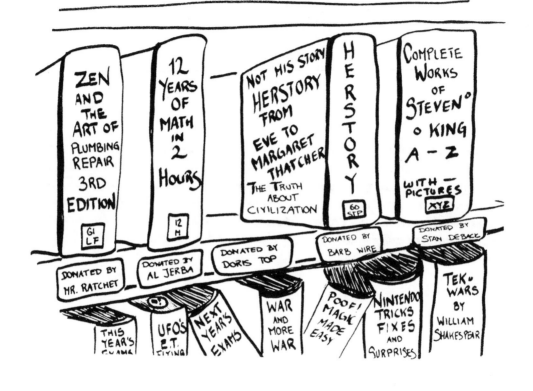

Nifty Idea 92

Books for the Library

Start a program in which the graduating students purchase a new book for the library's fiction section. Use a letter to solicit. Make arrangements with a local bookstore for a discount. Develop criteria for the student to use in making a selection, but encourage students to donate a book that they enjoyed or which they found encouraging or worthwhile. Make sure that the donation is recognized by a plaque in the front of the book. It's a great way to keep new and popular books in the collection.

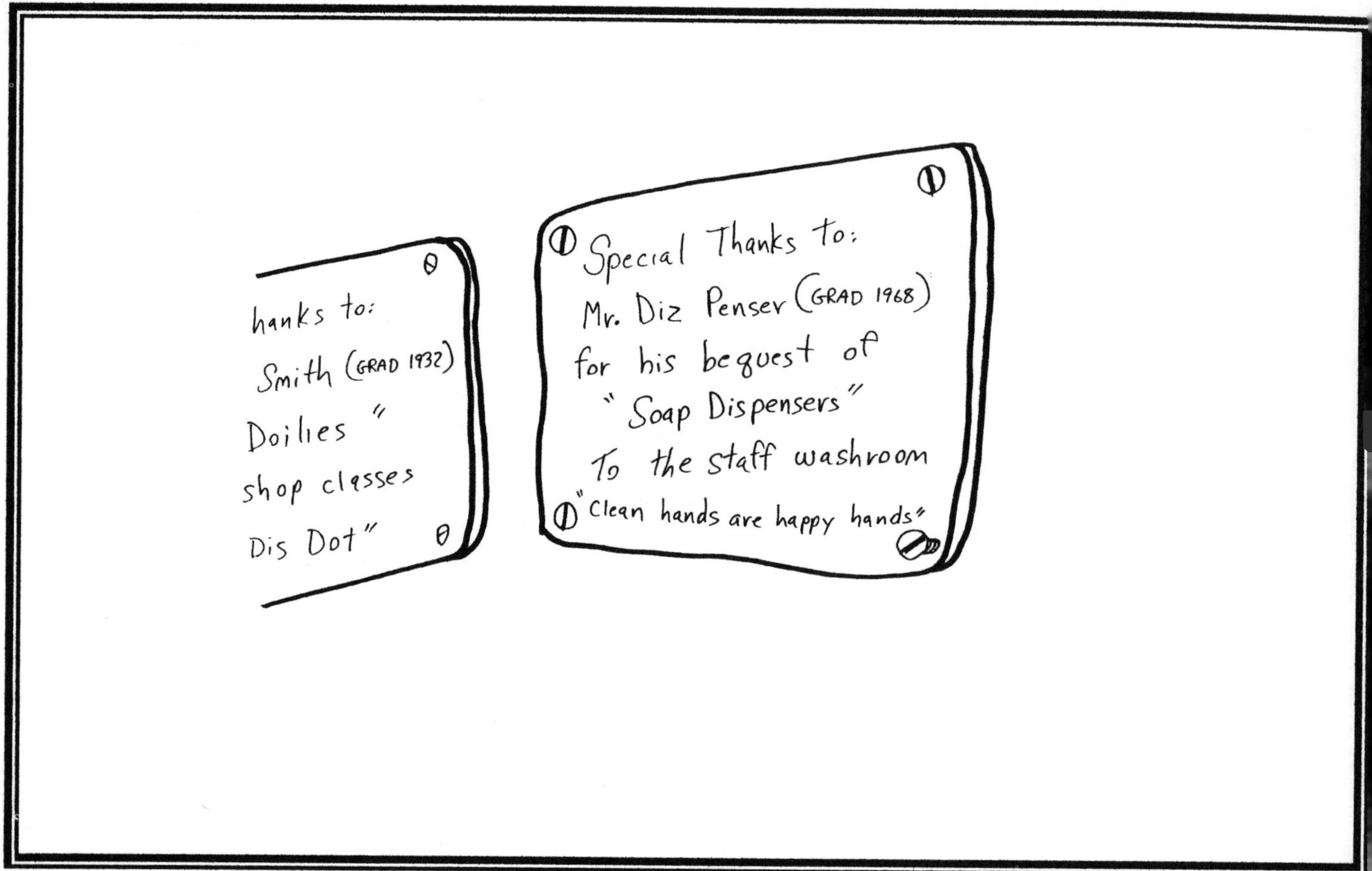
hanks to:
Smith (GRAD 1932)
Doilies "
shop classes
Dis Dot"
Special Thanks to:
Mr. Diz Penser (GRAD 1968)
for his bequest of
"Soap Dispensers"
To the staff washroom
"Clean hands are happy hands"

Nifty Idea 93

Ask for a Bequest

A different sort of idea with the potential for huge benefits! Take the opportunity to give tours at graduation reunions, for those who would like to visit their old school. Plant the seed for a bequest to the school from the alumni for the school's scholarship fund, or for any other good cause. Offer to reward the donor with a scholarship in their name or a plaque to be hung in the school. That will provide a legacy. As people get older, (at least in my case), they think about their legacy, and there is nothing better than a commitment to education.

Building a sense of team in the staff

Nifty Idea 94

Hand Out a Scratch Ticket

Looking for something just before the end of term at Christmas? Buy a scratch and win ticket for each staff member. Give them out after class on the last day around a cup of eggnog and a cheese tray. They are an inexpensive way of saying thank you and who knows, someone might make a little extra Christmas spending money. Insist that the scratching be done in the staff room. Applaud all winners.

Nifty Idea 95

Friday Treats

Even with a large staff, you can organize Friday treats. Staff members take turns bringing baked goods, a plate of cookies, cupcakes, squares, or whatever, on Friday for lunchtime. It's a morale booster and a little something to look forward to. Offer a prize, if you like, for the treat of the day.

Staff Dinner

Your staff might be interested in a gourmet meal at a local restaurant. Consider a formal evening out for staff members. It can be no-host, just a relaxing dinner together. It's a means of bringing people together in a different type of setting. Theme nights work, as do progressive dinners and specially ordered meals in a nice restaurant. Even if not all staff is interested, those who come will have a great time.

Nifty Idea 97

Christmas Toys

Pick out a couple of simple wooden toy projects. Work with your woodwork teacher and set up an assembly line with interested staff members on a Saturday. Build a few dozen of the toys: helicopters, cars, trucks, etc. Give the completed toys to the Salvation Army or some other charity for distribution at Christmas. Feel the internal satisfaction. Issue a press release with a couple of photos if you like. What's fun is getting staff members into the woodshop, working with their hands, and perhaps discovering a new hobby.

Nifty Idea 98

Creating Groups for Group Work

Quite often you need staff to work in groups. Here's a way to create groups that provides some activity and levity for the staff. Have the staff sit in chairs in a circle and you stand in the middle. Announce that you will be making a statement and that everyone the statement applies to is invited to stand and take another seat. Then say something like, "My friends are wearing something white" (or earrings, or glasses, etc.) Everyone wearing white needs to stand and find another chair. Whoever is left in the center, makes the next statement, and you continue until the seating pattern is quite mixed up. You'll know when to stop by the statements made. With you in the center, count off to create groups. A good classroom exercise as well!

Nifty Idea 99

Staff Appreciation

Teachers give up a lot of their own time to make school teams and clubs successful. The reality is that they are often out-of-pocket for expenses too. Encourage team members to send a card (it can be made simply with a computer program) to the teacher's family thanking them for their understanding and support. You'll only be out the cost of a stamp, and you'll bring a lot of gratitude to your programs and schools.

Nifty Idea 100

Staff golf shirts

From time to time, see if staff is interested in buying school golf shirts, sweaters, or windbreakers. There is no greater statement of pride in a school than wearing the school colors and logo. It's easy marketing and advertising.

Nifty Idea 101

Take the Secretaries With You

Sometimes, teachers will get the opportunity to visit other schools. You'll be doing yourself and your secretaries a favor if they get to visit other schools with you. In addition to being a nice change of pace, there is the opportunity for them to pick up some techniques that they might try back at home and increase the office efficiency. Sometimes small ideas can save a lot of time and money.

ABOUT THE AUTHOR

William (Bill) Reid is presently the District Principal for Distance Education, International Programs and Technology in School District 8 (Kootenay Lake). He resides in Nelson, British Columbia. Born in Scotland, Bill grew up in Ontario where he recieved an Honours BA in English Literature at Trent University, which was quickly followed by a Bachelor of Eduction degree at Queensí University.

Bill and his wife, Brenda, began teaching careers in Fort St. John, British Columbia. His working career has been at the junior and senior high school levels as an English teacher, Department Head, Vice-Principal and, after a move to Nelson, BC, a high school principal.

Bill furthered his education by completing a Masters Degree in Educational Adminstration at Simon Fraser University and a Ph.D. in Educational Leadership at Gonzaga University.

When time permits, Bill speaks at conferences on a variety of topics such as team building, site-based management, time management, and educational change.